HAL•LEONARD
Classical
PLAY-ALONG™

Volume 15

Wolfgang Amadeus
MOZART
(1756-1791)

Violin Concerto in G Major, KV 216

The Hal Leonard Classical Play-Along™ series allows you to work through great classical works systematically and at any tempo with accompaniment.

Tracks 2-4 on the CD demonstrate the concert version of each movement. After tuning your instrument to Track 1 you can begin practicing the piece. Using the Amazing Slow-Downer technology included on the CD, you can adjust the recording to any tempo you like without altering the pitch. (Note that when using Amazing Slow-Downer, the CD will stop after each track instead of playing continuously.) The full cadenzas are played only in the concert version.

- Track No. 1 – tuning notes
- Track numbers in circles ◯ – concert v...
- Track numbers in diamonds ◆ – play...

CONCERT VERSION

Alexander Trostyansky, Violin

Russian Philharmonic Orchestra Moscow

Konstantin Krimets, Conductor

ISBN 978-1-4234-6254-5

HAL•LEONARD®
CORPORATION
7777 W. BLUEMOUND RD. P.O. BOX 13819 MILWAUKEE, WI 53213

In Australia Contact:
Hal Leonard Australia Pty. Ltd.
4 Lentara Court
Cheltenham, Victoria, 3192 Australia
Email: ausadmin@halleonard.com.au

Visit Hal Leonard Online at
www.halleonard.com

CONCERTO

for Violin in G Major, KV 216

I ②

W. A. Mozart (1756 - 1791)
Edited by H. Scherz

2

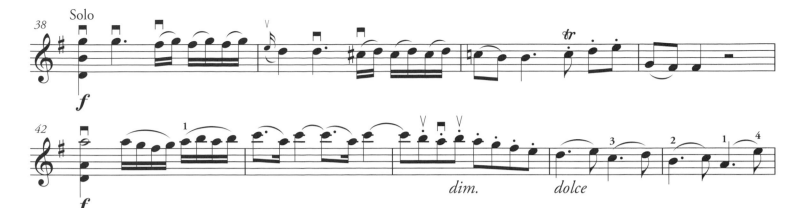

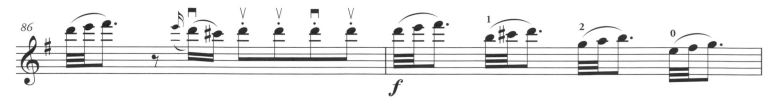

Cadenza

7

II ③

III ④

Tutti

Andante

Allegretto

13

Tempo primo

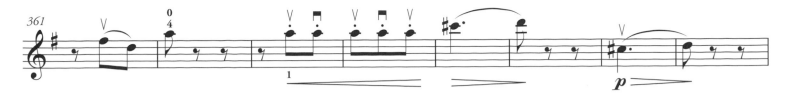